Olympic Greats

OLYMPIC BASKETBALL LEGENDS

MARTIN GITLIN

BLACK RABBIT BOOKS

Bolt is published by Black Rabbit Books
P.O. Box 3263, Mankato, Minnesota, 56002.
www.blackrabbitbooks.com

Jen Besel, editor; Catherine Cates, designer;
Omay Ayres, photo researcher

Library of Congress Cataloging-in-Publication Data
Names: Gitlin, Marty, author.
Title: Olympic basketball legends / by Martin Gitlin.
Other titles: Basketball legends | Bolt (North Mankato, Minn.)
Description: Mankato, Minnesota : Bolt is published by Black Rabbit Books, 2021. | Series: Bolt. Olympic greats | Includes webography. | Includes bibliographic references and index. | Audience: Ages 8-12 years | Audience: Grades 4-6
Identifiers: LCCN 2019027605 (print) | ISBN 9781623102647 (Hardcover) | ISBN 9781644663608 (Paperback) | ISBN 9781623103583 (eBook)
Subjects: LCSH: Basketball players—Rating of—Juvenile literature. | Basketball players—Records. | Olympic athletes—Juvenile literature. | Olympics—History—Juvenile literature. Classification: LCC GV885.1 .G57 2021 (print) | LCC GV885.1 (ebook) | DDC 796.323—dc23
LC record available at https://lccn.loc.gov/2019027605
LC ebook record available at https://lccn.loc.gov/2019027606

Printed in the United States. 2/20

All statistics are through the 2016 Olympic Games.

Image Credits

Alamy: Jack Sullivan, 13, 24, 28–29 (medal); PA Images, 16; SPUTNIK, 8; Xinhua, 12; AP Images: Charlie Neibergall, 7 (main); Eric Gay, 1; HANS DERYK, 25; Robert Kozloff, 15; Getty: Harry E. Walker/MCT, 19; ullstein bild, 21 (b); Newscom: ADREES LATIF, 26; BOB LEVERONE, 22 (main); Brian Cassella, 4–5; Christophe Elise/Icon SMI 483, Cover; Shutterstock: Cherdchai charasri, 32; Christos Georghiou, 10–11(balls), 20–21 (bkgd); EFKS, 10–11 (court); mipan, 3; mtkang, 7 (texture); Nata-Art, 6, 14, 18, 23 (medals); NWM, 28 (ticket); onot, 31; Paul Crash, 9, 17, 22, 27 (rings); twitter.com: Bleacher Report, 20(t); www.is.fi: Koripallo, 23 (main)
Every effort has been made to contact copyright holders for material reproduced in this book. Any omissions will be rectified in subsequent printings if notice is given to the publisher.

CONTENTS

USA
5
Rio2016

CHAPTER 1

Amazing ATHLETES

They are quick and strong. They can pass the ball and score. Basketball players are some of the best athletes in the world. The best of the best play in the Summer Olympics.

The Summer Olympics are held every four years. Countries send their top players to compete. Check out these amazing Olympians.

CHAPTER 2

Powerful PLAYERS

Carmelo Anthony

Carmelo Anthony is a powerful **forward**. He scored a total of 336 points in the Olympics. That's more than any other American man.

Anthony's Top-Scoring Olympic Games

37 POINTS
August 2, 2012
vs. Nigeria

31 POINTS
August 10, 2016
vs. Australia

21 POINTS
August 22, 2008
vs. Argentina

20 POINTS
August 4, 2012
vs. Lithuania

18 POINTS
August 10, 2012
vs. Argentina

Before the Olympics, **national** teams play tournaments. The winners go to Olympics. In the Games, teams play rounds. Winners move on. The losers are done. The top four teams play up to eight games.

• • • • Sergey Belov

The United States won every gold medal in basketball until 1972. That year, Sergey Belov and his team put a stop to that. Belov had a great **jump shot**. And he was quick dribbling to the basket. He scored 20 points to beat the United States in the final game.

COMPARING COUNTRIES

Men's basketball has been an Olympic sport since 1936. Women have competed since 1976. Here's the medal count by country.

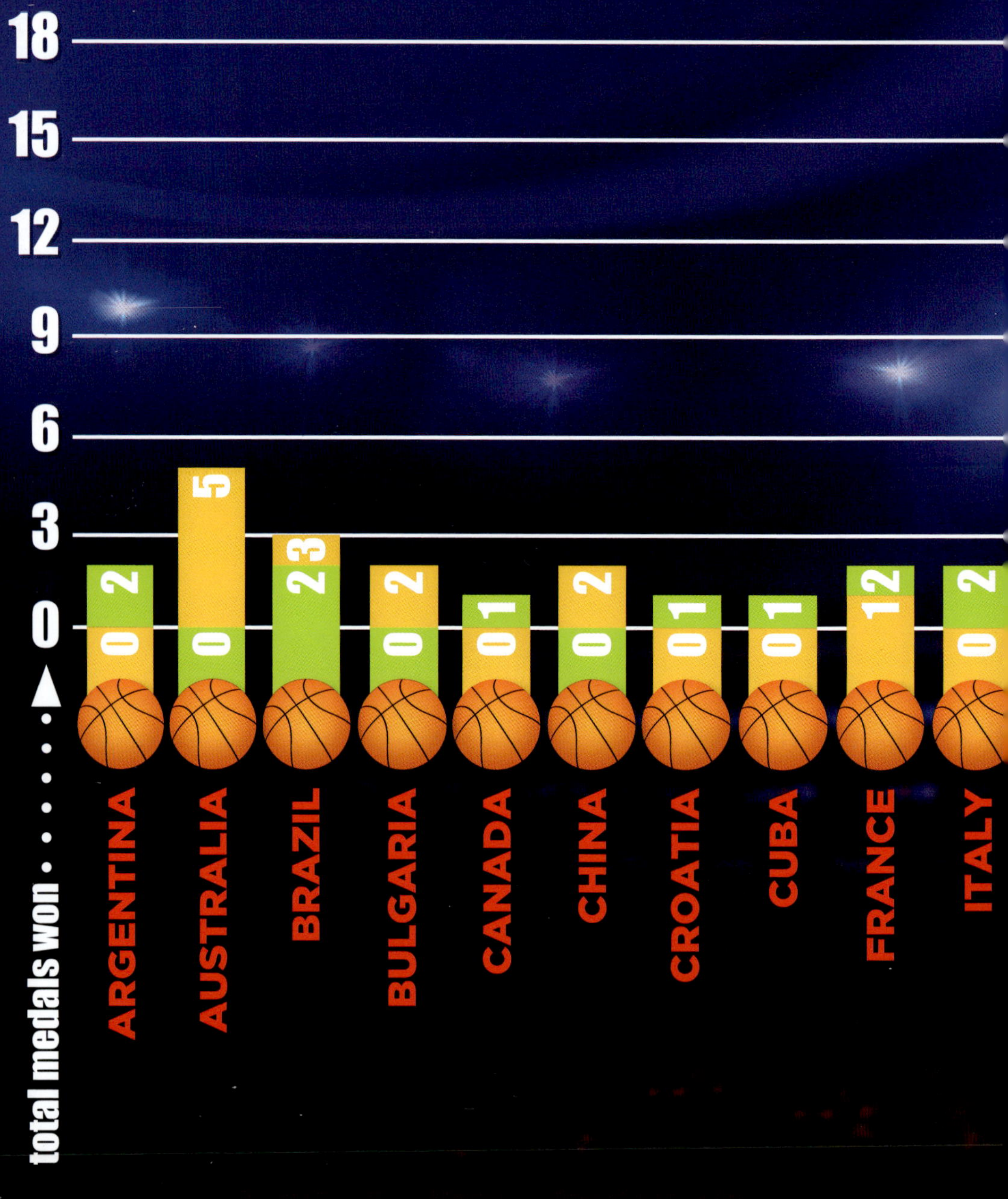

Men's Teams
Women's Teams
* These countries no longer exist.
LITHUANIA
3
0
MEXICO
1
0
RUSSIA
2
1
SERBIA
1
1
SOUTH KOREA
1
0
SOVIET UNION*
9
3
SPAIN
4
1
UNITED STATES
18
10
URUGUAY
2
0
YUGOSLAVIA*
6
2

Durant is a 3-point star. He holds the Olympic record for making the most 3-point shots.

Kevin Durant

Kevin Durant is an amazing scorer. And he is a strong **rebounder** and passer. The forward led the U.S. team to two gold medals. He **averaged** nearly 20 points per game in 2016.

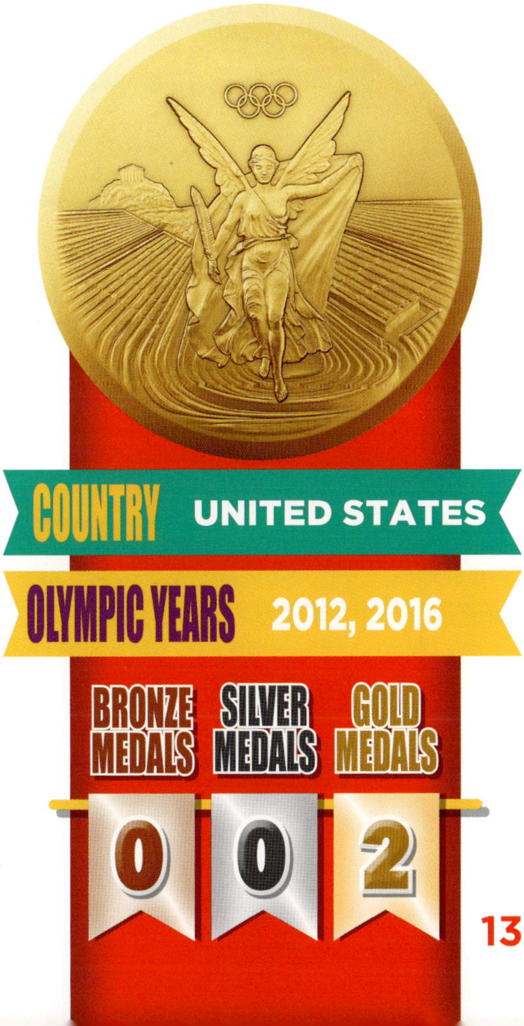

Teresa Edwards

Teresa Edwards was a powerful player. She used her quick speed on the court. Edwards holds records for being the youngest and oldest gold medalist in basketball.

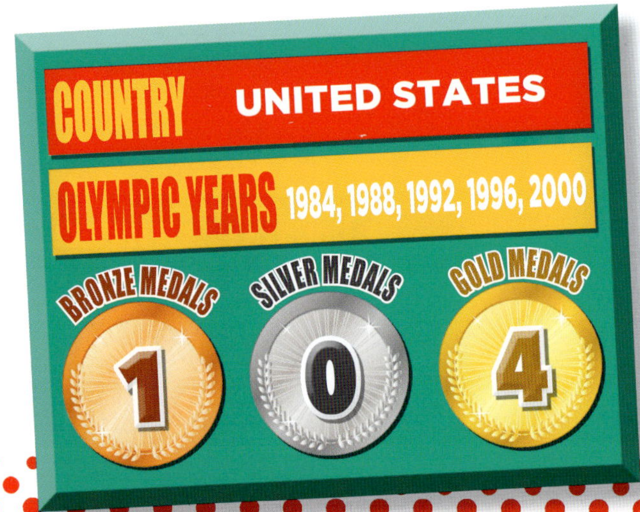

Edwards is the only female basketball player to win five medals.

Gaze averaged nearly 20 points in 40 Olympic games.

Andrew Gaze

Australia isn't known for winning in men's basketball. But one of its players was a star. Andrew Gaze was an amazing long-distance shooter. He finished his Olympic career with 789 total points.

Lauren Jackson

The U.S. team beat Australia in four straight Olympics. But Australia's Lauren Jackson didn't make it easy. She was an excellent shooter close to the basket. She played great **defense**. She was also a top rebounder.

Jackson's Highest Single-Game Olympic Rebounding Totals

August 9, 2012
vs. United States
17
rebounds

August 28, 2004
vs. United States
14
rebounds

August 17, 2008 vs. Russia	September 30, 2000 vs. United States	August 27, 2004 vs. Brazil
14 rebounds	**13** rebounds	**13** rebounds

FUN FACTS

NBA players weren't allowed in the Olympics at first. Officials didn't want **professionals** in the Games. The rule changed in 1992. That year, the United States **dominated**. The team was called "the dream team."

A new event started at the 2020 Olympics. Athletes now also play in 3x3 basketball.

THE FIRST OLYMPIC BASKETBALL GAMES WERE PLAYED OUTSIDE.

Lisa Leslie

Lisa Leslie was a great shooter and rebounder. And her record shows it. She played 32 games in the Olympics. She helped win them all.

Drazen Petrovic

Drazen Petrovic's team never won gold. But he never stopped scoring. He averaged 20 points in 23 games. Croatia probably wouldn't have any basketball medals without him.

Oscar Schmidt

Oscar Schmidt never won an Olympic medal. But no Olympian scored more. Schmidt could not be stopped in 1988. He scored 55 points in one game against Spain. That is an Olympic record.

All-Time Leading Scorers in Men's and Women's Basketball

MEN

Oscar Schmidt (Brazil) 1,093 points
Andrew Gaze (Australia) 789 points
Pau Gasol (Spain) 623 points

WOMEN

Lauren Jackson (Australia) 575
Janeth Dos Santos Arcain (Brazil) 535
Lisa Leslie (United States) 488

CHINA
7

Diana Taurasi

Diana Taurasi could do it all. She was a great shooter and passer. She played tough defense. And she led her team to four gold medals.

This **guard** improved with age. She scored 125 points in 2016. She only made 68 points in 2004.

CHAPTER 3

AVERAGE POINTS PER GAME

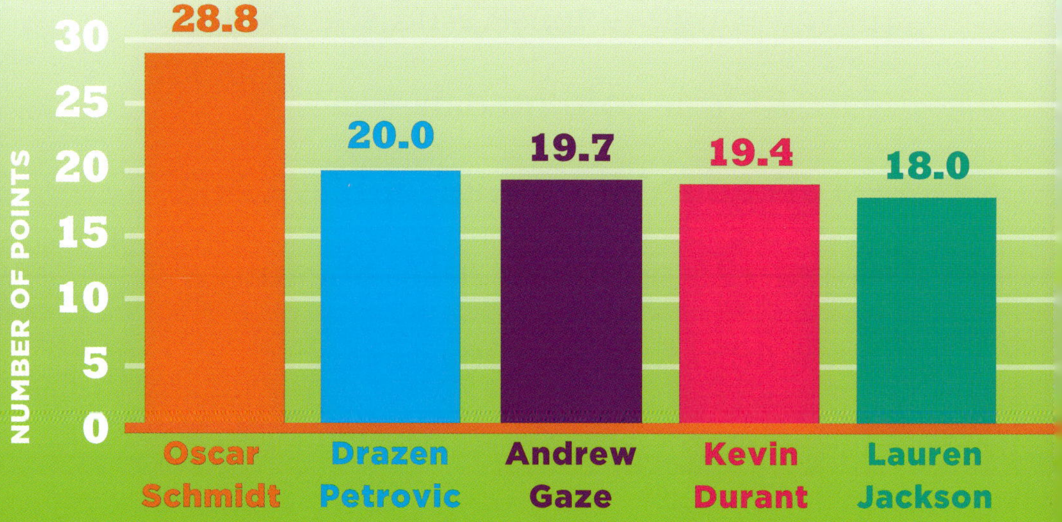

AVERAGE ASSISTS PER GAME

OLYMPIC BASKETBALL GREATS

4.5	TERESA EDWARDS
3.7	DIANA TAURASI
3.2	DRAZEN PETROVIC
3.1	KEVIN DURANT
2.9	SERGEY BELOV

STACK Them Up

Compare the stats of some of Olympic basketball's greats.

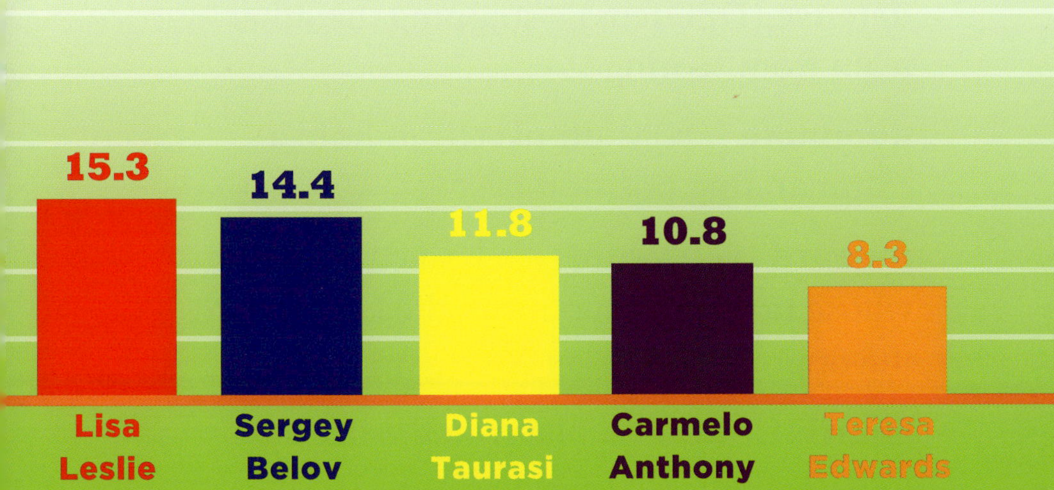

AVERAGE REBOUNDS PER GAME

10.7 Lauren Jackson

7.5 Lisa Leslie

5.5 Oscar Schmidt

TOTAL MEDALS

5 — TERESA EDWARDS

4 — CARMELO ANTHONY, LISA LESLIE, DIANA TAURASI, SERGEY BELOV, LAUREN JACKSON

3 — DRAZEN PETROVIC

average (AHV-rij)—a number that is calculated by adding quantities together and then dividing the total by the number of quantities

defense (DEE-fens)—stopping the other team from scoring

dominate (DOM-uh-neyt)—to hold a commanding position over

forward (FOR-wurd)—a basketball player whose main job is to move the ball toward the opponent's basket and try to score

guard (GARD)—a player in the backcourt in basketball

jump shot (JUMP SHAHT)—a shot made by jumping into the air and releasing the ball at the peak of the jump

national (NAH-shun-uhl)—relating to a country

professional (pro-FESH-uh-nuhl)—paid to participate in a sport or activity

rebounder (RE-bownd-uhr)—someone who takes possession of the ball after it bounces off the backboard or rim

LEARN MORE

BOOKS

Gitlin, Marty. *Kevin Durant: Basketball Star.* Biggest Names in Sports. Lake Elmo, MN: Focus Readers, 2017.

Herman, Gail. *What Are the Summer Olympics?* What Are ...? New York: Grosset & Dunlap, an imprint of Penguin Random House, 2016.

Mason, Tyler. *Incredible Olympic Records.* Incredible Sports Records. Mankato, MN: Child's World, 2016.

WEBSITES

Basketball
www.ducksters.com/sports/basketball.php

Olympic Basketball
www.olympic.org/basketball

Olympics Coverage from SI Kids
www.sikids.com/olympics

INDEX